ISBN 978-0-331-38682-0
PIBN 11116250

Historic, archived document

Do not assume content reflects current
scientific knowledge, policies, or practices.

TRADE IN
COTTON
FUTURES

Vol. 2	December 1941	No. 12

Issued Monthly

TRADE IN COTTON FUTURES

CONTENTS

SPECIAL CHARTS:
    Cotton: Total Stocks in Public Storage, "Free" Stocks,
    Government Owned and Loan Stocks, End of Month,
    October 1937 to November 1941.
        Spot and Futures Prices, Open Contracts and
    "Free" Stocks, End of Month, October 1937 to
    November 1941.

COTTON TOTAL STOCKS IN PUBLIC STORAGE, "FREE" STOCKS, GOVERNMENT OWNED AND LOAN STOCKS, END OF MONTH, OCTOBER 1937 TO NOVEMBER 1941

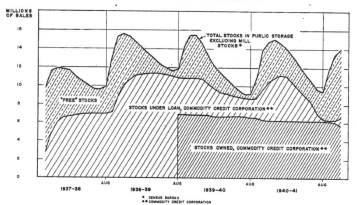

* CENSUS BUREAU
** COMMODITY CREDIT CORPORATION

SPOT AND FUTURES PRICES, OPEN CONTRACTS AND "FREE" STOCKS, END OF MONTH, OCTOBER 1937 TO NOVEMBER 1941†

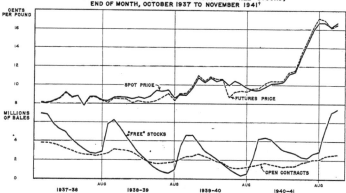

† AVERAGE PRICE AT TEN SPOT MARKETS DOMINANT FUTURES PRICE NEW YORK COTTON EXCHANGE
AND OPEN CONTRACTS ON ALL CONTRACT MARKETS

U. S. DEPARTMENT OF AGRICULTURE

1679 S – COMMODITY EXCHANGE ADMINISTRATION

Month.

1941 :
Aug. :

Sept.:

Oct. :

Nov. :

Dec. :

Table 1. - Cotton: Volume of trading and average daily open contracts,
by contract markets, all futures combined,
by months, 1941-42

Month	Volume of trading					Average daily open contracts			
	New York	New Orleans	Chicago	Total		New York	New Orleans	Chicago	Total
	100 bales	100 bales	100 bales	100 bales		100 bales	100 bales	100 bales	100 bales
1941									
Aug.	37,428	18,261.5	16.5	55,706.0		15,806	4,687	15	20,508
Sept.	48,990	24,701.5	27.0	73,718.5		16,762	5,200	11	21,973
Oct.	48,554	25,856.5	11.0	74,421.5		18,445	6,068	4	24,517
Nov.	26,480	10,726.0	4.5	37,210.5		18,734	6,349	6	25,089
Dec.	29,517	18,055.5	11.0	47,583.5		17,885	6,094	11	23,990

Table 2. - Cotton: Volume of trading and average daily open contracts,
all futures combined, on the New York Cotton Exchange,
by months, 1939-40 to 1941-42

Month	Cumulative volume of trading					Average daily open contracts		
	1929-30 : 1938-39 : Average	1939-40	1940-41	1941-42		1939-40	1940-41	1941-42
	100 bales	100 bales	100 bales	100 bales		100 bales	100 bales	100 bales
August	43,356	25,928	11,505	37,428		15,482	10,293	15,806
September	96,510	76,464	30,456	86,418		17,176	11,281	16,762
October	143,059	108,305	50,007	134,972		18,532	12,123	18,445
November	187,066	146,258	78,299	161,452		20,784	13,749	18,734
December	217,505	191,461	96,085	190,969		22,096	13,075	17,885
January	245,933	223,791	114,643			21,754	12,017	
February	282,354	241,867	128,868			19,574	11,034	
March	317,916	260,706	160,377			17,399	10,809	
April	356,327	284,137	184,128			15,185	11,492	
May	389,784	319,048	225,981			12,243	12,818	
June	432,156	342,870	261,537			10,602	13,562	
July	470,069	354,150	307,105			9,588	14,666	

Table 3. - Cotton: Volume of trading, New York Cotton Exchange,
December 1941

Date	All Futures	1941 Dec.	1942 Jan.	1942 Mar.	1942 May	1942 July	1942 Oct.	1942 Dec.	Other Futures
1941 December	100 bales	100 bales	100 bales	100 bales	100 bales	100 bales	100 bales	100 bales	100 bales
1	808	19	0	351	260	156	22		0
2	1,063	15	3	475	331	216	23		0
3	1,681	33 H	3	656	695	228	66		0
4	1,741	7	8	742	631	292	61		0
5	2,021	18	4	729	808	421	41		0
6	868	11	1	330	333	157	36		0
Sunday									
8	3,134 H	5	4	1,242 H	1,262 H	538 H	83 H		0
9	2,430	5	15	971	886	472	81		0
10	1,522	18	0	631	580	220	73		0
11	1,459	15	3	573	607	230	31		0
12	1,109	9	10	519	373	180	18		0
13	667	0 L	0	252	263	149	3 L		0
Sunday									
15	874	1	13	360	346	130	24		0
16	957	23	5	378	388	149	14		0
17	817		37	350	282	140	8	0	0
18	700		2	298	242	132	26	0	0
19	748		12	288	336	97	15	0	0
20	719		2	262	310	107	35	3	0
Sunday									
22	774		2	380	226	130	33	3	0
23	719		13	255	268	155	28	0	0
24	266 L		6	88 L	91 L	77	4	0	0
Holiday									
26	734		86 H	327	188	120	13	0 L	0
27	384		0	190	136	35 L	20	3	0
Sunday									
29	1,074		2	422	429	194	24	3	0
30	1,346		0	505	484	235	74	48 H	0
31	902		0 L	277	359	211	45	10	0
Total:									
Dec. 1941	29,517	179	231	11,851	11,114	5,171	901	70	0
Dec. 1940	17,786	1,863	124	5,889	4,787	3,457	1,569	97	0
*Dec. 1939	45,203	1,813	792	13,781	10,424	12,563	5,620	209	1

Abbreviations: H - High; L - Low.

* Figures represent totals of Old and New Contracts until Old Contract was
liquidated on July 17, 1940.

Table 4. - Cotton: Open contracts reported by clearing members,
New York Cotton Exchange,
December 1941

Date	1/ All Futures	1/ 1941 Dec.	1/ 1942 Jan.	1942 Mar.	1942 May	1942 July	1942 Oct.	1942 Dec.	Other Futures
1941 December	100 bales	100 bales	100 bales	100 bales	100 bales	100 bales	100 bales	100 bales	100 bales
1	18,247	135 H	177 H	7,726 H	6,978	2,924 L	307 L		0
2	18,223	123	176	7,653	6,967 L	2,985	319		0
3	18,327	94	176	7,671	7,018	3,022	346		0
4	18,321	89	170	7,565	7,059	3,074	364		0
5	18,283	81	170	7,403	7,110	3,148	371		0
6	18,352	79	169	7,362	7,183	3,182	377		0
Sunday									
8	18,353 H	79	168	7,260	7,208	3,234	404		0
9	18,288	74	168	7,119	7,232	3,272	423		0
10	18,203	54	168	6,978	7,272	3,298	433		0
11	18,069	43	168	6,934	7,212	3,281	431		0
12	18,061	31	170	6,889	7,239	3,300	432		0
13	18,095	31	170	6,870	7,241	3,352	431		0
Sunday									
15	18,064	31	161	6,856	7,223	3,349	444		0
16	17,946	0	156	6,768	7,215	3,363	444		0
17	17,880		124	6,712	7,224	3,372	448	0	0
18	17,845		124	6,622	7,243	3,409	447	0	0
19	17,816		121	6,585	7,246	3,414	450	0	0
20	17,794		120	6,524	7,288	3,395	465	2 L	0
Sunday									
22	17,632		119	6,376	7,263	3,401	468	5	0
23	17,526		108	6,318	7,234	3,408	453	5	0
24	17,497		103	6,302	7,218	3,415	454	5	0
Holiday									
26	17,365		17	6,209	7,251	3,428	455	5	0
27	17,331		17	6,136	7,282	3,437	453	6	0
Sunday									
29	17,261		14	5,992	7,345 H	3,446	456	8	0
30	17,185		14	5,846	7,306	3,479	487	53	0
31	17,050 L		14 L	5,748 L	7,238	3,479 H	510 H	61 H	0
Average: Dec. 1941:	17,885	67	125	6,786	7,204	3,303	426	17	0
Dec. 1940:	13,075	729	89	4,288	3,786	3,215	1,368	22	0
*Dec. 1939:	22,072	666	287	6,420	5,780	6,768	2,404	78	2

1/ Open contracts against which notices of delivery have been issued are not included.

* Figures represent average of Old and New Contracts combined until Old Contract was liquidated on July 17, 1940.

Table 5. - Cotton: High, low and closing prices per pound,
New York Cotton Exchange,
December 1941

Date		1941 December future				1942 January future		
	:	High	: Low :	Closing	:	High	: Low :	Closing
1941 December	:	cents	cents	cents	:	cents	cents	cents
1	:	16.20	16.09	16.15 N	:	---	---	16.17 N
2	:	16.25	16.16	16.25	:	16.25	16.22 L	16.31 N
3	:	16.51	16.31	16.50	:	16.40	16.37	16.61 N
4	:	16.65	16.56	16.61	:	16.72	16.63	16.66 N
5	:	16.82	16.57	16.82	:	16.75	16.58	16.84 N
6	:	16.66	16.66	16.74 N	:	16.82	16.82	16.82
Sunday	:							
8	:	16.98 H	16.95	16.75 N	:	17.05 H	16.93	16.84 N
9	:	16.75	16.49	16.37 N	:	16.60	16.56	16.49 N
10	:	16.21	15.98 L	16.07	:	---	---	16.27 N
11	:	16.40	16.17	16.43 N	:	16.45	16.45	16.57 N
12	:	16.55	16.43	16.42 N	:	16.65	16.65	16.56 N
13	:	---	---	16.21 N	:	---	---	16.36 N
Sunday	:				:			
15	:	16.29	16.29	16.38 N	:	16.55	16.48	16.54 N
16	:	16.65	16.35	16.51	:	16.61	16.61	16.56 N
17	:				:	16.50	16.41	16.37 N
18	.				:	16.40	16.40	16.42 N
19					:	16.54	16.50	16.48 N
20					:	16.60	16.60	16.55 N
Sunday								
22					:	16.62	16.61	16.62 N
23					:	16.68	16.65	16.65 N
24					:	16.66	16.65	16.65 N
Holiday								
26	:				:	16.63	16.56	16.55 N
27	.				:	---	---	16.56 N
Sunday					:			
29					:	16.69	16.58	16.71 N
30	:				:	---	---	16.90 N
31	:				:	---	---	16.98 N
	:				:			
Average: Dec. 1941	:	16.53	16.39	16.44	:	16.61	16.56	16.58

Abbreviations: H - High; L - Low; N - Nominal.

Table 5. - Cotton: High, low and closing prices per pound,
New York Cotton Exchange,
December 1941 -- Continued

Date	1942 March future			1942 May future		
	High	Low	Closing	High	Low	Closing
1941 December	cents	cents	cents	cents	cents	cents
1	16.47	16.32 L	16.39	16.54	16.41 L	16.50
2	16.54	16.39	16.53-54	16.67	16.50	16.67
3	16.82	16.58	16.81-82	16.95	16.70	16.94-95
4	17.00	16.85	16.88	17.14	16.96	17.01-02
5	17.12	16.75	17.06-07	17.25	16.86	17.20
6	17.08	16.93	17.05-08	17.20	17.08	17.19-20
Sunday						
8	17.34	16.65	17.06	17.48 H	16.74	17.16-17
9	17.25	16.52	16.71-73	17.37	16.63	16.82
10	16.75	16.45	16.53-55	16.89	16.56	16.66-68
11	16.95	16.58	16.82-85	17.07	16.74	16.97
12	17.08	16.84	16.88-90	17.22	16.97	17.03-04
13	16.79	16.62	16.63	16.92	16.75	16.75-78
Sunday						
15	16.95	16.75	16.86	17.10	16.89	17.01
16	16.98	16.75	16.90-91	17.13	16.88	17.05
17	16.88	16.76	16.76	17.01	16.91	16.91-92
18	16.84	16.76	16.80-81	16.99	16.90	16.95-96
19	16.96	16.85	16.86	17.09	16.99	17.01
20	17.01	16.89	16.92-94	17.16	17.03	17.06-07
Sunday						
22	17.06	16.98	17.01	17.20	17.12	17.13-14
23	17.09	17.03	17.04-05	17.22	17.15	17.19-20
24	17.07	17.01	17.05	17.22	17.16	17.19
Holiday						
26	17.03	16.95	16.95	17.18	17.08	17.08-09
27	17.00	16.93	16.96	17.15	17.08	17.11
Sunday						
29	17.15	16.98	17.11	17.29	17.14	17.24
30	17.31	17.20	17.30-31	17.45	17.33	17.45
31	17.34 H	17.18	17.26-28	17.47	17.33	17.42
Average: Dec. 1941	16.99	16.79	16.89	17.13	16.92	17.03

Table 5. - Cotton: High, low and closing prices per pound,
New York Cotton Exchange,
December 1941 -- Continued

Date	1942 July future			1942 October future		
	High	Low	Closing	High	Low	Closing
1941 December	cents	cents	cents	cents	cents	cents
1	16.54	16.44 L	16.53	16.60	16.48 L	16.55
2	16.68	16.51	16.68	16.71	16.55	16.70
3	17.00	16.73	16.99-17.00	17.03	16.76	17.03
4	17.20	17.02	17.05-08	17.23	17.03	17.08
5	17.32	16.90	17.28-29	17.34	16.94	17.28 N
6	17.29	17.17	17.24-25	17.31	17.18	17.30
Sunday						
8	17.52 H	16.75	17.17-20	17.58 H	16.85	17.20
9	17.37	16.64	16.80-82	17.30	16.72	16.88
10	16.89	16.58	16.68-72	16.93	16.58	16.77 N
11	17.11	16.79	17.02-03	17.16	16.85	17.08 N
12	17.26	17.03	17.07-10	17.26	17.10	17.15
13	17.00	16.80	16.80	17.03	16.90	16.85 N
Sunday						
15	17.14	16.92	17.04-05	17.18	16.95	17.08 N
16	17.16	16.90	17.10	17.16	16.88	17.10 N
17	17.05	16.93	16.93-95	17.05	16.99	16.99 N
18	17.02	16.95	17.01	17.00	16.94	16.97
19	17.13	17.02	17.06	17.12	17.03	17.03 N
20	17.20	17.07	17.10-13	17.19	17.08	17.12
Sunday						
22	17.24	17.16	17.17 N	17.23	17.16	17.20
23	17.27	17.19	17.23	17.24	17.20	17.23 N
24	17.27	17.21	17.25	17.25	17.25	17.25
Holiday						
26	17.23	17.15	17.15	17.23	17.15	17.15-16
27	17.20	17.15	17.16 N	17.20	17.12	17.18
Sunday						
29	17.35	17.19	17.30	17.35	17.21	17.30
30	17.50	17.39	17.49 N	17.53	17.40	17.52-53
31	17.51	17.39	17.49	17.54	17.44	17.49 N
Average: Dec. 1941	17.17	16.96	17.07	17.18	16.99	17.10

Table 5. - Cotton: High, low and closing prices per pound,
New York Cotton Exchange,
December 1941 -- Continued

Date		1942 December future			
	:	High	: Low	: Closing	:
1941 December	:	cents	cents	cents	:
1	.				
2					
3					
4					
5					
6					
Sunday 8					
9					
10	:	.			
11					
12					
13					
Sunday 15		.			
16					
17	:	---	---	16.99 N	:
18	:	---	---	16.98 N	:
19	:	---	---	17.04 N	:
20	:	17.18	17.18 L	17.14 N	:
Sunday 22	:	17.24	17.22	17.23 N	:
23	:	---	---	17.26 N	:
24	:	---	---	17.28 N	:
Holiday 26	:	---	---	17.18 N	:
27	:	17.22	17.19	17.20 N	:
Sunday 29	:	17.36	17.34	17.34	:
30	:	17.50	17.44	17.54 N	:
31	:	17.54 H	17.46	17.53 N	:
	:				:
Average: Dec. 1941	:	17.34	17.30	*	:

* Average not computed for lack of actual sales on close.

Table 6. - Cotton: Volume of trading and average daily open contracts, all futures combined, on the New Orleans Cotton Exchange, by months, 1939-40 to 1941-42

Month	Cumulative volume of trading					Average daily open contracts		
	1929-30 1938-39 Average	1939-40	1940-41	1941-42		1939-40	1940-41	1941-42
	100 bales	100 bales	100 bales	100 bales		100 bales	100 bales	100 bales
August	14,365	4,151.5	1,841.0	18,261.5		2,424	1,615	4,687
September	31,400	14,160.5	4,762.0	42,963.0		2,671	1,816	5,200
October	46,237	19,599.5	7,876.0	68,819.5		3,332	2,153	6,068
November	60,247	27,233.5	12,819.5	79,545.5		3,480	2,497	6,349
December	70,030	38,672.0	15,439.5	97,601.0		3,181	2,491	6,094
January	79,215	46,324.0	19,361.5			3,400	2,467	
February	90,602	50,020.5	22,348.5			3,266	2,100	
March	101,539	54,730.5	29,677.5			2,722	1,829	
April	112,881	59,457.0	36,533.0			2,377	2,039	
May	123,390	67,915.0	51,450.0			1,896	2,879	
June	135,764	72,527.5	67,279.5			1,690	3,721	
July	148,281	74,957.0	91,555.0			1,606	4,606	

Table 7. - Cotton: Volume of trading, New Orleans Cotton Exchange,
December 1941

Date	All Futures	Future							
		1941 Dec.	1942 Jan.	1942 Mar.	1942 May	1942 July	1942 Oct.	1942 Dec.	Other Futures
1941 December	100 bales	100 bales	100 bales	100 bales	100 bales	100 bales	100 bales	100 bales	100 bales
1	399.5	5	1	185	157.5	46	5		0.0
2	459.5	22	.0	130.5	204	94.5	8.5		.0
3	1,140	104 H	.0	480.5	429.5	113	13		.0
4	1,136	10	.0	436	513	151.5	25.5		.0
5	1,327	1.5	.0	508.5	693	112	12		.0
6	624	.0	.0	209.5	333.5	74	7		.0
Sunday									
8	2,216.5H	4	2	935 H	950.5H	278 H	47 H		.0
9	1,902	.0	3	763.5	908.5	194	33		.0
10	1,096.5	4	16 H	469	476	115	16.5		.0
11	857.5	2	.0	311	441	92.5	11		.0
12	842.5	.0L	.0	277.5	492.5	56.5	16		.0
13	476.5	1	.0	175.5	245	46	9		.0
Sunday									
15	399	1.5	.0	137	218	40.5	2		.0
16	582	10	.0	218.5	303.5	49	1		.0
17	332.5		6	114	174.5	32	4	2	.0
18	352.5		.0	110.5	184.5	54.5	3	.0	.0
19	387.5		.0	142.5	202	35	6	2	.0
20	383		.0	120.5	212.5	43	7	.0	.0
Sunday									
22	509.5		1	194.5	200.5	109.5	2	2	.0
23	184.5		.0	69	95	17.5L	2	1	.0
24	168 L		.0	77	73 L	18	.0L	.0	.0
Holiday									
26	358		4	155	174.5	22	.5	2	.0
27	232.5		.0	60 L	101	58.5	12	1	.0
Sunday									
29	429.5		.0L	132	196.5	91	7	3 H	.0
30	696		4	191	351.5	127.5	22	.0L	.0
31	563.5		1	228	216.5	106.5	11	.5	.0
Total:									
Dec. 1941	18,055.5	165.0	38.0	6,831.0	8,547.5	2,177.5	283.0	13.5	0.0
Dec. 1940	2,620.0	304.5	5.0	812.5	679.0	491.5	308.5	19.0	0.0
*Dec. 1939	11,438.5	313.5	198.0	3,194.0	2,837.5	3,297.5	1,542.5	55.5	0.0

* Figures represent totals of Old and New Contracts until Old Contract was
liquidated on July 17, 1940.

Table 8. - Cotton: Open contracts reported by clearing members,
New Orleans Cotton Exchange,
December 1941

Date	1/ All Futures	1/ 1941 Dec.	1/ 1942 Jan.	Future 1942 Mar.	1942 May	1942 July	1942 Oct.	1942 Dec.	Other Futures
1941 December	100 bales	100 bales	100 bales	100 bales	100 bales	100 bales	100 bales	100 bales	100 bales
1	6,706.5	215.5H	31.5	2,795	2,794	728.5L	142 L		0.0
2	6,728.5H	199.5	31.5	2,795 H	2,802 H	756	144.5		.0
3	6,511	38.5	31.5	2,731	2,786.5	778	145.5		.0
4	6,527	33	31.5	2,757.5	2,735.5	807	162.5		.0
5	6,390	31.5	31.5	2,666	2,691	803.5	166.5		.0
6	6,320.5	31.5	31.5H	2,636	2,663	790	168.5		.0
Sunday									
8	6,204	30.5	30.5	2,556.5	2,548	853.5	185		.0
9	6,216	25.5	30.5	2,491.5	2,608.5	870	190		.0
10	6,162.5	25.5	28.5	2,480.5	2,546 L	890.5	191.5H		.0
11	6,091	25.5	28.5	2,431	2,560.5	861	184.5		.0
12	6,128.5	25.5	28.5	2,407.5	2,625.5	860	181.5		.0
13	6,136	25	28.5	2,393.5	2,651	857	181		.0
Sunday									
15	6,081.5	15.5	28.5	2,369.5	2,638	850	180		.0
16	6,031.5	.0L	28.5	2,349.5	2,616	857	180.5		.0
17	6,025.5		22.5	2,342.5	2,623.5	855.5	179.5	2.	.0
18	6,013		22.5	2,315.5	2,617.5	876	179.5	2	.0
19	5,943.5		22.5	2,237	2,624.5	874	183.5	2	.0
20	5,888.5		22.5	2,202	2,611.5	870	180.5	2 L	.0
Sunday									
22	5,875.5		21.5	2,162	2,568	938.5	181.5	4	.0
23	5,824		21.5	2,124.5	2,554	936.5	182.5	5	.0
24	5,799		21.5	2,072	2,585	933	182.5	5	.0
Holiday									
26	5,820.5		19.5	2,034	2,641.5	938.5	182	5	.0
27	5,800.5		19.5	2,026.5	2,634	938.5	177	5	.0
Sunday									
29	5,755		19.5	1,981	2,633.5	938	178	5	.0
30	5,717.5L		17	1,930	2,606	972	187.5	5	.0
31	5,747		17 L	1,881.5L	2,625	1,033 H	185	5.5H	.0
Average: Dec. 1941:	6,094.0	51.5	25.5	2,352.5	2,638.0	872.0	176.0	4.0	0.0
Dec. 1940:	2,491.0	166.5	6.5	763.5	702.5	662.5	277.5	6.0	0.0
*Dec. 1939:	3,181.0	148.0	56.5	892.0	778.0	945.0	414.0	12.5	0.0

1/ Open contracts against which notices of delivery have been issued are not
included.

* Figures represent average of Old and New Contracts combined until Old Contract
was liquidated on July 17, 1940.

Table 9. - Cotton: High, low and closing prices per pound,
New Orleans Cotton Exchange,
December 1941

Date		1941 December future				1942 January future		
	:	High	Low	Closing	:	High	Low	Closing
1941 December	:	cents	cents	cents	:	cents	cents	cents
1	:	16.21	16.12 L	16.19B-21A	:	---	---	16.22B
2	:	16.30	16.24	16.32B-34A	:	---	---	16.35B
3	:	16.59	16.32	16.55B-58A	:	---	---	16.60B
4	:	16.67	16.60	16.58B-62A	:	---	---	16.69B
5	:	---	---	16.77B-84A	:	---	---	16.86B
6	:	---	---	16.75B-84A	:	---	---	16.86B
Sunday	:				:			
8	:	16.84 H	16.30	16.70B-80A	:	17.00	17.00	16.85B
9	:	---	---	16.38B-44A	:	16.58	16.58	16.56B
10	:	16.32	16.17	16.21B-28A	:	16.54	16.33 L	16.30B-35A
11	:	16.58	16.56	16.54B-59A	:	---	---	16.65B
12	:	---	---	16.52B-60A	:	---	---	16.64B-69A
13	:	16.50	16.50	16.17B	:	---	---	16.36B
Sunday	:				:			
15	:	---	---	16.40B-50A	:	---	---	16.59B
16	:	16.55	16.43	16.55	:	---	---	16.64B-70A
17	:				:	16.57	16.56	16.43B
18	:				:	---	---	16.52B
19	:				:	---	---	16.53B
20	:				:	---	---	16.65B
Sunday	:				:			
22	:				:	16.68	16.68	16.68B
23	:				:	---	---	16.70B
24	:				:	---	---	16.70B
Holiday	:				:			
26	:				:	16.65	16.63	16.59B
27	:				:	---	---	16.63B
Sunday	:				:			
29	:				:	---	---	16.74B
30	:				:	16.92	16.86	16.96B
31	:				:	17.00 H	17.00	16.93B
	:				:			
Average: Dec. 1941	:	16.51	16.36	16.50	:	16.74	16.70	*

Abbreviations: A - Asked; B - Bid; H - High; L - Low; N - Nominal.

* Average not computed for lack of actual sales on close.

Table 9. - Cotton: High, low and closing prices per pound,
New Orleans Cotton Exchange,
December 1941 -- Continued

Date		1942 March future				1942 May future		
	:	High	Low	Closing	:	High	Low	Closing
1941 December	:	cents	cents	cents	:	cents	cents	cents
1	:	16.50	16.36 L	16.44-45	:	16.58	16.45 L	16.55
2	:	16.58	16.46	16.58	:	16.72	16.56	16.70-72
3	:	16.86	16.62	16.85-86	:	16.97	16.75	16.96
4	:	17.05	16.89	16.92-93	:	17.19	17.00	17.06
5	:	17.16	16.77	17.09-10	:	17.30	16.89	17.24-25
6	:	17.11	17.00	17.09	:	17.25	17.15	17.23
Sunday	:							
8	:	17.40	16.72	17.08-09	:	17.53	16.80	17.19-20
9	:	17.29	16.56	16.74-78	:	17.40	16.67	16.88-90
10	:	16.82	16.49	16.58	:	16.94	16.60	16.73-75
11	:	16.97	16.66	16.93-94	:	17.13	16.81	17.06-07
12	:	17.12	16.88	16.95	:	17.29	17.02	17.08-09
13	:	16.82	16.64	16.67-69	:	16.94	16.80	16.82-83
Sunday	:							
15	:	16.98	16.80	16.90	:	17.13	16.93	17.03-04
16	:	17.03	16.80	16.95	:	17.18	16.94	17.08-09
17	:	16.94	16.80	16.80	:	17.08	16.95	16.95-97
18	:	16.89	16.80	16.89	:	17.04	16.95	17.03-04
19	:	16.98	16.90	16.90-91	:	17.14	17.05	17.05
20	:	17.05	16.93	17.02	:	17.20	17.07	17.17
Sunday	:							
22	:	17.12	17.03	17.05	:	17.27	17.18	17.18-19
23	:	17.13	17.08	17.10-11	:	17.26	17.21	17.25
24	:	17.12	17.06	17.10	:	17.28	17.21	17.25
Holiday	:							
26	:	17.08	16.99	16.99	:	17.24	17.13	17.13-14
27	:	17.06	16.97	17.03	:	17.21	17.12	17.16-18
Sunday	:							
29	:	17.19	17.05	17.13-14	:	17.34	17.20	17.28
30	:	17.37	17.23	17.35	:	17.50	17.38	17.49-50
31	:	17.40 H	17.25	17.33	:	17.53 H	17.42	17.47-48
	:				:			
Average Dec. 1941	:	17.04	16.84	16.94	:	17.18	16.97	17.08

Table 9. - Cotton: High, low and closing prices per pound,
New Orleans Cotton Exchange,
December 1941 -- Continued

Date		1942 July future				1942 October future		
	:	High	Low	Closing	:	High	Low	Closing
1941 December	:	cents	cents	cents	:	cents	cents	cents
1	:	16.62	16.50 L	16.58	:	16.77	16.68 L	16.74B-77A
2	:	16.78	16.58	16.75-78	:	16.95	16.85	16.93-95
3	:	17.04	16.79	17.02-04	:	17.20	17.00	17.20
4	:	17.25	17.07	17.13-14	:	17.37	17.23	17.28B-30A
5	:	17.38	16.98	17.33	:	17.53	17.34	17.49B
6	:	17.33	17.23	17.30	:	17.45	17.40	17.46B-48A
Sunday	:				:			
8	:	17.58	16.87	17.26	:	17.77 H	17.23	17.43B-47A
9	:	17.43	16.70	16.90	:	17.49	16.93	17.08B-10A
10	:	16.92	16.62	16.75	:	17.10	16.84	16.95B
11	:	17.15	16.86	17.11	:	17.32	17.08	17.31B-33A
12	:	17.31	17.12	17.14B-15A	:	17.50	17.30	17.33B-35A
13	:	16.98	16.82	16.89	:	17.17	17.00	17.05B-07A
Sunday	:				:			
15	:	17.18	16.99	17.09B-10A	:	17.28	17.28	17.27B-30A
16	:	17.22	17.00	17.13	:	---	---	17.30B-33A
17	:	17.13	17.01	17.01	:	17.26	17.18	17.16B
18	:	17.05	17.00	17.09B-10A	:	17.16	17.16	17.23B
19	:	17.17	17.11	17.09B-10A	:	17.34	17.25	17.25B
20	:	17.23	17.13	17.21	:	17.33	17.33	17.35B-37A
Sunday	:				:			
22	:	17.31	17.22	17.23B-25A	:	17.35	17.35	17.38B
23	:	17.31	17.28	17.30	:	17.48	17.48	17.43B
24	:	17.31	17.27	17.30B-31A	:	---	---	17.43B
Holiday	:				:			
26	:	17.27	17.21	17.18B-19A	:	---	---	17.31B
27	:	17.26	17.18	17.23	:	17.37	17.36	17.36B-38A
Sunday	:				:			
29	:	17.40	17.27	17.36	:	17.44	17.44	17.49B-51A
30	:	17.57	17.43	17.56-57	:	17.73	17.64	17.72B-74A
31	:	17.59 H	17.48	17.55	:	17.75	17.68	17.74B-75A
Average: Dec. 1941	:	17.22	17.03	17.14	:	17.35	17.22	17.30

Table 9. - Cotton: High, low and closing prices per pound,
New Orleans Cotton Exchange,
December 1941 -- Continued

Date	1942 December future			
	High	Low	Closing	
1941 December	cents	cents	cents	
1				
2				
3				
4				
5				
6				
Sunday				
8				
9				
10				
11				
12				
13				
Sunday				
15				
16				
17	17.21	17.21 L	17.21B	
18	---	---	17.26B-28A	
19	17.34	17.34	17.28B	
20	---	---	17.38B	
Sunday				
22	17.46	17.46	17.43B	
23	17.50	17.50	17.47B-50A	
24	---	---	17.47B	
Holiday				
26	17.50	17.50	17.37B-40A	
27	17.45	17.45	17.42B-44A	
Sunday				
29	17.59 H	17.59	17.53B-56A	
30	---	---	17.74B-77A	
31	---	---	17.77B-80A	
Average: Dec. 1941	17.44	17.44	*	

* Average not computed for lack of actual sales on close.

- - - - - - - -

According to reports to the Commodity Exchange Administration, 66,855
bales of cotton were tendered in settlement of the 1941 December future on the
New York and New Orleans Cotton Exchanges. The tenders represented 42.1 percent
of the total contracts open at the close of business November 24, 1941, the day
preceding first notice day for the December future. On the New York Cotton Exchange there were 54,023 bales delivered and 12,832 on the New Orleans Cotton
Exchange. Deliveries on the New York and New Orleans contracts at Houston
amounted to 29,783 bales or 44.5 percent of the total and at Galveston 36,116
bales or 54.0 percent of the total. On the New York contract only, 956 bales
were delivered at New Orleans.

Strict Middling, Strict Low Middling and Strict Middling Spotted were
the principal grades delivered and accounted for 13,679 bales or 20.5 percent,
11,859 bales or 17.7 percent and 10,088 bales or 15.1 percent of the total tendered.

Of the 573 notices of delivery issued at New York, 282 notices or 49.2
percent of the total were stopped without transfer, 118 notices or 20.6 percent
were transferred one time, 80 or 14.0 percent, two times, 48 or 8.4 percent,
three times, 16 or 2.8 percent, four times, 11 or 1.9 percent, five times,
11, six times, 4, seven times, 2, nine times, and 1, ten times. In New Orleans,
89 notices or 65.9 percent were stopped without transfer, 30 were transferred
one time, 11, two times, 4, three times and 1, five times.

The average number of qualities appearing on notices issued at New York
was 2.5. The number of qualities ranged from one to nineteen. On a cumulative
basis 510 notices or 89.1 percent had five qualities or less and 569 notices or
99.3 percent had ten qualities or less. Notices issued at New Orleans contained
one to thirteen qualities and averaged 2.9 qualities per notice. Out of 135
notices issued, 117 or 86.7 percent had five qualities or less and 130 notices or
96.4 percent had 10 qualities or less.

Comparison of certificated stocks at the beginning and end of the
delivery period indicated a net decrease of 19,464 bales with a total of 100,479
bales in stock on December 22, 1941.

Detailed information with regard to deliveries on the 1941 December
future is given in tables 10 to 14 which follow:

Table 10. - Grade and staple of cotton delivered in settlement of the
1941 December future on the New York and New Orleans Cotton Exchanges

Grade	7/8"	29/32"	15/16"	31/32"	1" and up	Total
	Bales	Bales	Bales	Bales	Bales	Bales
White						
Middling fair	0	0	0	0	0	0
Strict good middling	0	0	0	0	0	0
Good middling	2	7	16	0	5,187	5,212
Strict middling	358	296	179	96	12,750	13,679
Middling	407	541	1,555	1,087	3,231	6,821
Strict low middling	1,025	976	3,366	2,759	3,733	11,859
Low middling	1,152	1,174	2,534	1,029	1,361	7,250
Extra White						
Good middling	0	0	0	0	820	820
Strict middling	0	0	0	0	7,225	7,225
Middling	0	0	0	0	2,674	2,674
Strict low middling	0	0	0	0	0	0
Low middling	0	0	0	12	9	21
Spotted						
Good middling	195	157	340	219	295	1,206
Strict middling	2,086	1,184	3,599	1,672	1,547	10,088
Total	5,225	4,335	11,589	6,874	38,832	66,855

Table 11. - Distribution of deliveries in settlement of the
1941 December future by delivery point on the
New York and New Orleans Cotton Exchanges

Delivery point	New York	New Orleans	
		100-bale contract	50-bale contract
	Bales	Bales	Bales
Houston	25,962	3,821	---
Galveston	27,105	9,011	---
New Orleans	956	---	---
Mobile	---	---	---
Savannah	---	---	---
Charleston	---	---	---
Norfolk	---	---	---
New York	---	---	---
Total	54,023	12,832	---

	Number of notices	Percent of notices	Number of transfers	Number of notices	Percent of notices	Number of transfers	Number of notices	Percent of notices	Number of transfers
0	282	49.2	0	89	65.9	0	---	---	---
1	118	20.6	118	30	22.2	30	---	---	---
2	80	14.0	160	1	8.2	22	---	---	---
3	48	8.4	144	4	3.0	12	---	---	---
4	16	2.8	64	---	---	---	---	---	---
5	11	1.9	55	1	.7	5	---	---	---
6	11	1.9	66	---	---	---	---	---	---
7	4	.7	28	---	---	---	---	---	---
9	2	.3	18	---	---	---	---	---	---
10	1	.2	10	---	---	---	---	---	---
Total	573	100.0	663	135	100.0	69	0	---	0

1/ A transfer occurs when a notice of delivery is received by a "long" and then applied on a liquidating sale made on the same trading day either before or after receipt of the notice within a limited period prescribed by the rules of the exchange.

Table 13. - Number of qualities 1/ on notices issued in
settlement of the 1941 December future on the
New York and New Orleans Cotton Exchanges

Number of qualities on each notice	New York		New Orleans			
			100-bale contract		50-bale contract	
	No. of notices	Percent	No. of notices	Percent	No. of notices	Percent
1	300	52.4	52	38.5	---	---
2	85	14.8	41	30.4	---	---
3	53	9.3	8	5.9	---	---
4	52	9.1	6	4.5	---	---
5	20	3.5	10	7.4	---	---
6	28	4.9	2	1.5	---	---
7	10	1.7	6	4.5	---	---
8	7	1.2	2	1.5	---	---
9	7	1.2	2	1.5	---	---
10	7	1.2	1	.7	---	---
11	1	.2	3	2.2	---	---
12	1	.2	1	.7	---	---
13	---	---	1	.7	---	---
19	2	.3	---	---	---	---
Total	573	100.0	135	100.0	---	---
Average qualities per notice	2.5	---	2.9	---	---	---

1/ A quality is the combination of grade and staple expressed as one unit;
thus, bales alike in both grade and staple are of one quality.

Table 14. - Certificated stocks of cotton by grade and staple [1]
on first notice day and last delivery day
showing net change in stocks

(Bales)

Grade	November 25, 1941					Total	December 22,					Total	Net change
White													
MF	---	---	---	---	---	---	---	---	---	---	---	---	
SGM	---	---	---	---	---	---	---	---	---	---	---	---	
GM	161	172	190	68	2,988	3,579	158	166	152	32	2,937	3,445	
SM	1,825	1,906	4,556	3,451	14,244	25,982	1,510	1,580	3,227	1,499	11,093	18,909	– 7,
M	3,258	3,466	8,168	6,079	9,153	30,124	2,962	2,763	5,986	3,695	5,955	21,361	– 8,
SLM	1,744	1,850	6,024	4,430	6,587	20,635	1,659	1,416	4,893	3,725	5,771	17,464	– 3,
LM	482	391	1,122	584	1,106	3,685	904	1,474	3,393	1,233	1,218	8,222	+ 4,
Extra White													
GM	---	---	---	---	1,193	1,193	---	---	---	---	1,187	1,187	
SM	---	4	---	---	16,153	16,157	---	4	---	---	13,489	13,493	– 2,
M	2	---	2	2	5,500	5,506	2	---	2	2	4,683	4,689	
SLM	5	---	---	---	---	20	5	---	---	---	---	20	
LM	2	---	---	---	3	9	2	---	---	---	3	9	
Spotted													
GM	339	276	650	383	435	2,083	330	250	524	336	340	1,789	
SM	2,069	1,439	3,291	1,899	2,272	10,970	2,058	1,364	2,801	1,681	1,987	9,891	– 1,
Total	9,887	9,503	24,011	16,906	59,636	119,943	9,590	9,025	20,986	12,213	48,665	100,479	–19,

[1] Certificated stocks reported by the New York Cotton Exchange in daily market reports.
[2] Grades are abbreviated by initials; see Table 10 for grades.

Chic
L.
Rc
14

Knn
L
8

Min
J
£

Nov
7
I

Nu

Pc

S

COMMODITY EXCHANGE ADMINISTRATION
U. S. Department of Agriculture
J. M. Mehl, Chief

Field Offices	Markets Supervised
Chicago, Illinois L. A. Fitz, In charge Room 1200, Board of Trade Building 141 West Jackson Boulevard	Chicago Board of Trade Chicago Mercantile Exchange Chicago Open Board of Trade Milwaukee Grain and Stock Exchange
Kansas City, Missouri L. E. Wolf, In charge 854 Board of Trade Building	Kansas City Board of Trade Merchants' Exchange of St. Louis
Minneapolis, Minnesota Joseph B. Withers, In charge 510 Chamber of Commerce Building	Duluth Board of Trade Minneapolis Chamber of Commerce
New Orleans, Louisiana W. D. Espy, In charge Room 306, New Orleans Cotton Exchange Building	Memphis Merchants' Exchange Clearing Association New Orleans Cotton Exchange
New York, New York George H. Baston, In charge Room 602, New York Cotton Exchange Building	New York Cotton Exchange New York Mercantile Exchange New York Produce Exchange Wool Associates of the New York Cotton Exchange, Inc.
Portland, Oregon Harold I. Hollister, In charge Room 716, Lewis Building	Portland Grain Exchange Seattle Grain Exchange
San Francisco, California Richard F. Shortell, Acting in charge Room 650, 821 Market Street	Los Angeles Grain Exchange San Francisco Grain Exchange

- 0 -

SPECIAL FEATURES

January   None

February   Cotton: Closing price of dominant future on the New York Cotton
               Exchange, Ten Spot Market average price of Middling 15/16", and   Chart
               Parity Price, middle of month, August 1939 to January 1942.....   1751

March   None

April   None

May   None

June   None

Trade in cotton futures
United States. Commodity Exchange Authority;United States. Com
CAT11084093_022
U S Department of Agriculture, National Agricultural Library

[22] tradeincottonfut212unit

Dec 04, 2013

CPSIA information can be obtained
at www.ICGtesting.com
Printed in the USA
BVHW091628121118
532888BV00015B/513/P